You Don't Die - You Just Change Channels!

A common sense guide to God our Creator and Eternity in Heaven

Chuck Swartwout

A Feedback Book[tm]

You Don't Die - You Just Change Channels!

Visit our Website at
http://ChuckSwartwout.com
for more information.

ISBN: 978-1519619372

Cover by Stark Artisan, LLC

About the Book Cover

The painting on the front cover of this book is a copy of an original 22" x 25" watercolor painted by my wife. It is titled "Kachina Impressions," and was inspired by the Hopi Indian Kachina dolls. These dolls have great spiritual significance in the Hopi culture.

Kachina dolls are figures typically carved from cottonwood root, which act as messengers between humans and the Spirit World. When I was visiting the Hopi Indian reservation many years ago, I purchased this from Pat Lanza, the man who carved it. This beautiful doll is named the Deer Kachina.

When you look at the black and white picture of the Deer Kachina, you need to use your imagination, because in reality it is magnificently colored. Just imagine many of the hues that are in the painting on the front cover of my book superimposed on this beautifully carved doll. I felt that it was very appropriate to include this picture here, because this book is about communication with the Spirit World.

Gretchen loved to paint the mountains! She was a plein-air artist who especially enjoyed the beauty of transparent watercolor. She has been described as one who saw the beauty of nature, of design, of color, through rose-colored glasses. It was the beauty of nature, of design, of color, that inspired and influenced her painting.

Gretchen earned her BA degree from Ohio Wesleyan University and studied further at the Cleveland Institute of Art and at Arizona State University. Over the years she took workshops with many fine artists and teachers: Bill Schimmel, Doug Greenbow, Dick Phillips, Jim Scott, Tony van Hasselt, Judi Wagner, Jeanne Dobie, Robert Wood, Eric Weigardt, Gretchen Lopez and others. Her work can be found in collections in the USA and abroad.

To Gretchen, the love of my life on this earth for 54 years, and now forever in the future when I join her in Heaven!

Table of Contents

Introduction

Why I Wrote This Book

This is the first major book that I've ever written, and I'm excited about it. I hope that it will be the first in a series of two or three books that I will write. When I tell you that I am 94 years old, you may think that I'm either nuts or a dreamer to think that I can accomplish all that at an age where some people don't want to commit themselves to buying green bananas. Well, I don't think I'm nuts, but I will admit to being a dreamer. I think nearly everyone who's accomplished anything in this world has been a dreamer.

I find that most everyone is interested in learning more about eternal life, and this is especially true the older you get. It is my impression that we would all like proof of eternal life in the Spirit World. There has been a lot of research on this subject, and one of the reasons that I decided to write this book is that I felt I had some "common sense" views that I have not seen covered elsewhere. One thing I think is important about my common sense views is that I don't believe they conflict with most views that people currently have on this subject. For example, there are many people who believe in the inerrancy of the bible, while there are many other people who don't believe that any of the stories in the bible are literally true. I am not taking sides on this issue. I respect everyone's views, and I hope that my common sense ideas will serve to reinforce your present views, whatever they may be.

As I said, I am a dreamer, and along those lines I can't help thinking of Martin Luther King, Jr. He became famous for his phrase, "I have a dream," and just think of the tremendous impact that dream has had on our world in reducing prejudice against black people. We've made great progress in this regard, but we still have a long way to go. Today, as I write these words, we're seeing a great deal of conflict between black and white people in communities throughout the United States. This must end, because God created us all to be equal, and if we respect God we will make sure that this is the way we behave as human beings.

Before I end this book I will share with you

my dream for eliminating all wars in the world! This is a very specific plan, which was proven during World War II. Stay tuned for the exciting climax in Appendix 1.

I was brought up in a traditional Protestant Sunday school, and when we were kids we learned about Heaven and many other things about our faith. Of course, we accepted what we learned without question, and this was wonderful. Today, I still try to see everything in our magnificent universe through the eyes of a child, but with increased knowledge and education, I am aware that some of the things I automatically accepted as a child are being questioned by many people. This has caused me to re-examine my thinking in regard to the Afterlife.

When my wife died very suddenly after 54 years of a wonderful marriage, the idea of understanding Heaven and the Spirit World became very important to me. I truly believe that we will all be reunited in the Spirit World after we pass on, because this is what my Christian religious faith has taught me. But I am also seeking to learn more about the Spirit World, as I seek "proof " that Heaven does exist. This has caused me to do a great deal of research, and I now believe that I have proven to my satisfaction that the Spirit World which we call "Heaven" does truly exist. As you read on, I believe you will understand my common sense approach to this question. While I lean heavily on my experience solving creative problems in the field of Engineering, I can also call on my later experience as a motion picture producer, in which I created many TV commercials and films designed to inform and motivate people.

A number of books have been written on this subject and many authors claim to have "proof" of an Afterlife. One man, James Randi, has for many years offered a one million dollar prize for anyone who could prove that an Afterlife truly exists. Randi had a career as a magician until he retired at age 60, at which time he set up the James Randi Educational Foundation. He has set up a rather difficult set of conditions that must be met in order to provide proof of an Afterlife, and so far nobody has been able to claim the one million dollar prize. Of course, you should be aware that Randi is an atheist. If you would like to learn more about James Randi there is an excellent Wikipedia article about him.

One thing I have found is that it is not easy to write a book. I have had to study a tremendous amount of written material, which I found to be helpful in formulating my own ideas. It takes a lot of time and dedication to do this, but I am a great believer that God works through people, and this keeps me motivated. I believe he is working through me, and I see this as an awesome responsibility. I certainly don't want to let God down!

While doing my research, I came across the following quotation:

> *"Believe nothing, no matter where you read it, or who said it, not even if I have said it, unless it agrees with your own reason and common sense"*
>
> *- Buddha*

I am not a Buddhist, but I have found this to be a useful guide while doing my research, and I also think that it is very applicable to thinking about what is going on in our world today. We seem to be really lacking in common sense as we try to solve the many problems facing our world. The problem with "common sense" is that it may not be very common. It should probably be called "uncommon sense"!

One thing I want to make very clear is that when I use words like "mankind" or "layman" these should be broadly interpreted to include both men and women. For example, if you look in the dictionary it defines words such as "chairman" as the person that presides over a meeting. It does not refer to male or female.

So, welcome to my book. I believe that my approach to gaining greater understanding of the Afterlife is different than many of the other approaches I have studied, and I hope that the insights I provide will be helpful to you. After you have finished reading it, I hope you will feel as confident as I am that there will be a place for you in Heaven, and that we can all look forward to the joy of being united with our loved ones.

Chapter 1

Who Is This Chuck Swartwout Guy?

First, I want to tell you how to pronounce my name. In my last name the second "w" is silent, so the name is pronounced "Swartout."

Before going into the main text of this book, I want to tell you a little bit about me. I think it's very important in reading a work of non-fiction to evaluate the writer's credentials, because it is helpful for you to know where he is coming from in order to determine if what he says is meaningful for you. This chapter is fairly long, but please bear with me, because I think that it's important for you to know some of the key influences that motivated my life.

I was trained as an electrical engineer and a great deal of my career involved the design of feedback control systems. A creative design engineer has a great advantage, in that he knows from practical experience if his concepts are correct. For example, if you design a car and you do a good job, it will perform flawlessly for its user. On the other hand, if there are design flaws, you will learn about it the minute the car breaks down or crashes. Of course, when something goes wrong, a good engineer can make corrections to eliminate this problem in the future.

When I started writing this book I was going to call it "An Engineer's Guide to God Our Creator." Later, I decided to call it "A Common Sense Guide to Our Creator" because I thought more of my readers would relate to this title. Everyone likes to think that they have Common Sense!

Before we go any further, you should know that I have never read the Bible all the way through from beginning to end, but I have studied many portions of it, first as a young child in Sunday School, and later at a men's Bible study class at my church, the Church of the Red Rocks in Sedona, Arizona.

My intention in writing this book is to write it in a "conversational" style, just as if you and I were sitting down together for a chat over cups of coffee. I have avoided the use of sophisticated words or abstract scientific terms, because I really didn't want you to have to read it with a dictionary in your lap. As I've said before, this is a "Common Sense" book, written in easy to understand language, so it will be easy for you to read. Also, it is a fairly short book, so you should be able to read it easily in one or two sittings.

In order to help give this book a "conversational" tone, I have avoided writing using a computer keyboard. Instead, I am using a voice-actuated computer program called "Nuance Dragon Naturally Speaking." This way I can chat into a microphone, and the computer will print out what I am saying. It does an amazingly good job of transcribing the voice into the printed word, and only minor corrections are required here and there during the editing process.

Now you might ask how this can be a "conversation" when I am the only one doing the talking. Well, this brings me to the point where I will tell you about the long-range plan for this book, which I think is rather unique. You may have noticed that on the title page I refer to this as "A Feedback Book™." This means that when you have finished reading the book, you will have an opportunity to feed back your comments to me by sending them to my website. I am hopeful that I will receive many comments, as I believe that the collective wisdom of all of my readers will be an important contribution to our understanding of what is involved in the "Afterlife."

I would like this feedback to form the basis for a second book in this series. In Appendix 2: Book 2, I give you specific directions on how to provide this feedback to me. I think that sharing your insights will be a great contribution to our understanding of what is involved in the "After-life," and I am hopeful that I will hear from at least hundreds, or even thousands of readers.

So here are some details about my back-ground, to give you a better idea of exactly who I am and how I acquired the problem-solving skills that I'll bring to bear on my inquiry into the Life Hereafter.

When I was a youngster, my folks said that I was a "Curiosity Box," and that I was a boy who had screwdriver fingernails! I was always taking things apart to see what made them tick. I'm sure I ruined some things while I was exploring, but I had wonderful, loving parents who were very understanding, and who encouraged my curiosity. This actually had a big effect on my career later in life.

Here's the scoop about my formal education: I graduated from college in 1942 with a Bachelor's Degree in Electrical Engineering from Case Institute of Technology in Cleveland, Ohio. While I was at Case, I was nominated to Honorary Societies Sigma Xi, Eta Kappa Nu, and Theta Tau.

During World War II, I worked at the Radiation Laboratory at MIT on the design and testing of closed-loop feedback control systems. These were radar, servo-operated, automatic-tracking gun-laying systems. I worked closely with the Air Force, and as a civilian, I was in charge of flight testing a complex radar system that was installed in the P-61 night-fighter aircraft. Later on, I developed and flight tested the first K-band airborne rapid-scanning radar system.

After the war ended, I stayed at MIT, and in 1947 I obtained my Master's degree in Electrical Engineering. During that time I was working at the Servomechanisms Laboratory at MIT, and as part of my graduate school education I wrote a paper titled "History of the Development of Closed-Cycle Automatic Control of Industrial Processes" – not exactly a beach read!

When I left MIT, I then went to work for the Swartwout Company, a family-owned business in Cleveland, Ohio that was started by my grandfather around the start of the last century. When I started working for the Swartwout Company, they were already involved in the manufacture of control systems, which were largely operated by air pressure. Based on my wartime experience, I felt that most of these control systems could operate far more precisely if they were operated electronically. While at the Swartwout Company, I developed an all-electronic control system for use in the process industries.

The October 1990 issue of Control Engineering magazine gave my brother Ken and me the credit for developing the world's first all-electronic control system for use in chemical plants and oil refineries.

All of these projects involved "feedback" control systems, which were needed to run various industrial processes. There are two main categories of feedback systems: closed-loop feedback, and open-loop feedback. However, as I appreciated later, the principle of feedback is present in many areas in our everyday lives, and is critical to the solution of many problems facing our society. Today, virtually everyone is involved with feedback systems of one kind or another, even though they may not realize that this is the case.

An example of closed-loop feedback control is driving a car, which is something most of us do every day. When you are driving down the road there are usually two lines on the pavement that mark the lane in which you are to drive. With your eyes you observe the road ahead and detect any error between where your car is and where you want it to be. You then make the necessary correction with the steering wheel to keep your car within the space between the two lines. In the feedback control field this would be called "proportional control."

If you are a really good driver, however, you will also be using "derivative," or what some may call "anticipatory" control. This takes place when you observe the lines some distance ahead, and the road begins to curve. Before you actually get into the curve, you anticipate the need for making a correction, so you start to gently turn the steering wheel appropriately to keep the car within the two lines. This provides smoother action with your car and makes it possible to keep it well within the two lines without wandering back and forth from line to line. In more sophisticated kinds of control systems we also utilize what is called "integral" control. This allows for even finer tuning of the control process, for greater precision.

If you are a really skilled driver you can keep the car on course with very little movement of the steering wheel, and this contributes to a very smooth drive without a lot of jerking around. Whenever I drive behind another car, I tend to observe how well they are driving in regard to the two lines. I find that many drivers wander around a great deal between the lines, and often wander over the lines either off the road or across into the other lane. This means that they are not taking advantage of "derivative" or "anticipatory" control.

After working for the Swartwout Company for a number of years, the family business was sold, so I needed to look around for other opportunities that could take advantage of my experience. In 1960, my brother Ken and I went to work for

Motorola in Phoenix, Arizona. We worked for the relatively new Solid-State Systems Division. This was the time when so-called "integrated circuits" were just beginning to be developed. I was Chief Engineer of a new project to develop electronic process control systems for Motorola. My brother and I were successful in doing this, and in 1965 we introduced the Motorola Process Control Instrumentation line at the Instrument Society of America convention in New York City.

Later on, we had an amicable parting of the ways with Motorola, which meant that I needed to seek a new line of work. This time I decided to completely switch gears, and I went into the production of motion pictures! Our company, Swartwout Productions, produced many TV commercials and many so-called "sponsored" films. Most of these were designed to motivate people to take some important action, such as donating money or becoming involved in important causes.

Over the years, I had the unusual privilege of directing a number of well-known Hollywood actors. This list of actors included Jimmy Stewart, Dick Van Dyke, Kirk Douglas, and the famous radio newscaster Lowell Thomas. We were fortunate that Swartwout Productions won many national and international awards for these films. This phase of my life is covered in greater detail in the memoir of my life that I published in 2005.

In addition to complete films, we also produced many TV commercials. Swartwout Productions was listed in the 2005 Guinness Book of Records as the producer of the world's longest running TV commercial. We produced this commercial, titled "Thank You," for the Discount Tire Company of Scottsdale, Arizona. It features a little old lady returning a tire to the store by throwing it through the plate glass window of the Discount Tire dealership! It has aired every year since it was first aired in 1975.

One important thing that was common to nearly everything I have accomplished in life is that creativity was involved. I have always had a "can do" attitude about anything I tackled. I believe that there is always a better way to do almost everything in life, and it excited me to try and apply this skill to the pursuit of greater knowledge about the life hereafter.

When my wife, Gretchen, died suddenly in 2006, I felt very strongly that there had to be more to life than the time we spend physically on this earth, and my training as an engineer and scientist caused me to take an analytical approach to questions that I am now facing about the Afterlife. I am a Christian, and I had a fairly typical upbringing in the Protestant church, going to Sunday School as a kid – even though by the time

I was a teenager, that involved occasionally having my arm twisted a bit.

Also, I have always been very interested in music. I studied piano, pipe organ, saxophone, music composition, and singing, and my participation in the church choir helped to hold my interest in music. Today, I am composing classical music, and I feel that my inspiration to do this comes directly from God. I sense a greater answer to my prayers when I sit down at the keyboard to compose music, as compared to routine praying at other times.

There have been many books written about the Afterlife. One of the first ones I read was a book titled *The Afterlife Experiments*, written by Gary E. Schwartz, PhD, a professor at the University of Arizona. This was very convincing to me, as I believed Dr. Schwartz applied a scientific approach in his attempt to "prove" that an Afterlife truly existed. His book whetted my appetite to learn more about the Afterlife, and this led me to read many additional books and articles on the subject. I suppose that it was natural for me, because of my engineering background, to give special attention to books that looked at the Afterlife from a scientific point of view.

Next, I read a very meaningful article in the August 28, 2011 issue of USA Today. This was written by Dean Nelson, who directs the journalism program at Point Loma Nazarene University in San Diego. This article, titled "Why Certainty About God is Overrated," tells a fascinating account about John Polkinghorne, a British citizen, who was a world-class physicist before he retired at age 50, then decided to become a priest in the Anglican church in England. Subsequently, Dean Nelson, along with Karl Gilbertson, wrote a book titled *Quantum Leap*. This book, articles, and some significant websites are listed in the bibliography at the end of this book.

In writing my book, I have developed some additional insights that I hope will be helpful to you, my readers, as you further explore the mysteries of life. It is my belief that these insights will not conflict with the beliefs that most of you already have concerning the Afterlife. It is my goal to add some additional "common sense" beliefs to your present understanding of the Afterlife.

Chapter 2
A Love Story

Over 100 years ago in 1910, Victor Herbert wrote an operetta titled *Naughty Marietta*, and one of the popular songs from that operetta was "Ah Sweet Mystery of Life."

I was not living in 1910, but when I was a youngster in the 1920s, I remember gathering around the piano on Sunday evenings with our family and friends, singing the popular songs of the day. One of the ones that I loved best was "Ah Sweet Mystery of Life." In 1935, *Naughty Marietta* was made into a movie, featuring Nelson Eddy and Jeanette MacDonald, who were very popular singers at that time. This movie is available today on a DVD from Amazon.com. I'm sure that many of my older readers will remember this popular couple singing this very song.

Of course, my younger readers are probably more familiar with the song as sung by Madeline Kahn in the movie *Young Frankenstein*, in a very different (and very funny) context. But that's a different story.

The lyrics below have an important message for us today:

Ah! Sweet Mystery of Life

At last, I've found you.

Ah! At last I know the secret of it all.

For the longing, seeking,

Striving, waiting, yearning,

The burning hopes,

The joy and idle tears that fall.

For 'tis love and love alone,

The world is seeking.

And 'tis love and love alone,

That can repay.

'Tis the answer, 'tis the end and all of living,

For it is love alone that rules for aye.

In a very real sense these words really say it all. If we could just have love for all of God's creation, what a wonderful life it would be for everyone! If somehow I could convince myself and everyone reading this book – or, for that matter, the rest of the world – to somehow love everyone, I could end the book here, and all of our problems would be solved!

Today, we are living in the real world with real people. God gave us wills of our own to make decisions. We can make right decisions and we can make wrong decisions. I thank God that He gave us free will, as this is one thing that is totally unique to humankind. If we were not able to make our own choices, we would merely be puppets, and that would be no fun!

We are responsible for our own attitudes and behavior, so when we make poor choices and bad things happen, we can't blame God. We can, however, pray to God that He will give us the guidance and motivation to improve our behavior as time goes on, so that we can make more "right" decisions.

We can never be perfect, but this is something we should aim for. It's easy to subscribe to the concept that we should love everyone, but it may be difficult to put into practice, particularly if the people you are supposed to love are not like you, and may not share the same values that you have.

Recently I had an interesting experience that pertains to this discussion. I was at the Staples store in Sedona, buying some paper that was on sale. It was a very heavy box, and when I needed to put it into the shopping cart I found that it was too heavy for me to lift, so I asked for help from a nearby clerk. When I went to check out, I realized that this box would be too heavy for me to lift into the trunk of my car, so I asked the cashier if I could have some help. Very shortly a man came over and walked with me to my car and lifted the box into the trunk. He also asked how I would get the box out of the car when I got home, and I explained to him that my son could help with that.

I made some comment that at my age I just could not pick up something that heavy. He told me that he was about 40 years old, and then he asked me how old I was. When I said that I was 92 years old, he looked me straight in the eye and said, "Can I give you a hug?"

This was quite a surprise to me, but of course I said "Yes." I was surprised how much impact this had on me, especially as I thought about it a couple of days later. I finally decided that this heartwarming experience was a perfect example of a man putting his faith into action. It made me wonder whether or not I could do more to reach out to other people.

When I was a young boy, I didn't spend much time thinking about the meaning of life, but as I grew older I began to realize that life is truly a mystery. And as I moved forward on my faith journey, I became increasingly curious to unravel this mystery. Still, for many years I was pretty busy growing up, then marrying and raising a family with four children and eleven grandchildren, two new granddaughters by marriage, and a great-grandson. I didn't really give much thought to a life-hereafter, because I was very busy with a life-here-and-now. Besides, I was always going to live forever!

Then, just a few years ago, my wife died very suddenly, which reminded me of the mystery, and caused me to examine the reality of a life-hereafter. This has made me completely reevaluate my life, and where I stand with respect to God and His wonderful creation. As a result of this, I have done considerable research regarding an Afterlife. Perhaps "Afterlife" is not a good term to refer to the period after we physically die on this earth, as I believe we have a "continuing life" in the Spirit World.

It is the purpose of this book to present to you the results of my analysis, in the hope that it may be helpful to you as you ponder the mystery of your life, now and forever.

Chapter 3

The Mystery of Life Through the Ages

> *"As soon as man does not take his existence for granted, but beholds it as something unfathomably mysterious, thought begins."*
>
> *- Albert Schweitzer*

What a great thought expressed by the amazing Albert Schweitzer! This simple-but-profound insight has stimulated me to really explore the mysteries of life. Schweitzer was not only a great theologian and humanitarian, but he was also a superb pipe organist; I have an old 78 rpm recording of him playing Bach's Toccata and Fugue in D minor.

I think music and religion have a lot in common, in that both are mysterious, really defying our understanding. It's amazing that the mechanical vibration of air molecules can translate into beautiful music that has such a profound emotional impact on human beings. This is just one of the many gifts we have received from God, and I marvel at how it can enrich our lives!

Ever since mankind first appeared on the earth millions of years ago, people have had a profound desire to understand how the universe and this world were created. Moving up to early biblical times, I can picture the shepherds lying down at night in their fields, and gazing up at the stars. What a magnificent display they would have seen! Is it any wonder that they were able to come up with the imaginative names and pictures that became associated with all of the constellations? They had time to dream, and wonder, and make up stories that tried to explain the things that they could not possibly put into any sort of scientific context.

How much time do we have to dream today with all of the clutter that occupies our lives? I'm talking to you, Internet, Facebook, Twitter, and Text Messaging, etc.

Remember there was no TV, there was no radio, and most people did not know how to read or write. There was no "noise" to clutter up people's minds, except for the bleating of the sheep, and this was probably like music to the ears of the shepherds. To hear actual music, they had to make it themselves, on lyres, or simple flutes, or simply singing to the night sky.

Today, I wonder how much deep thinking occurs in the mind of a young person who is constantly involved in text messaging, video games, and continuous recorded music blasting into their earphones. Do they ever have a time of peace and quiet to really think, to wonder, to ponder the mysteries of life?

Early humans worshiped many gods, but today most religions are based on a concept of only one God who created our magnificent universe. What do we know about this one God that we worship? Well, the first answer that comes to my mind is, not very much. To be sure, we do have the Bible as one important source of information, and we have many scholars who have studied the Bible in great depth.

And then there are the scientists, who are continually searching for information that can be verified by experiments, designed to explain how our universe was created. It is important to understand that scientists are trained to speak in terms of "theories," which are carefully-considered interpretations of observable facts. As they accumulate more facts, scientists modify the theories or propose new ones. For example, Einstein's famous theory of relativity, which made nuclear energy possible and successfully predicted black holes, has been extensively updated due to ideas like quantum mechanics and string theory.

The important thing is to understand the difference between a theory and a fact. It is a fact that if you stand on the planet Earth and let go of a baseball, it will fall to Earth. We can measure how fast it falls, and observe that it always accelerates at the same rate. These are facts. Of course, we say this is due to gravity, but we don't have a clue as to what causes gravity. Exactly why the ball moves toward the much greater mass of the planet is a question that, despite many attempts at coherent theories, remains one of the biggest unanswered questions in science.

Chapter 4

Different Approaches to Learning About the Afterlife

As I see it, when we research the riddle of how the universe was created, and the prospect of an Afterlife, there are a number of different approaches that are currently being explored. Some of these are listed below:

1. *The Strictly Scientific Approach.* This is where we attempt to prove our theories by conducting verifiable and repeatable scientific experiments.

2. *The Biblical Approach*, or more broadly, the *Religious Approach*, which includes in-depth research on the impact of Jesus on our lives, if you are a Christian. If you are not a Christian, then you can study the written documentation that pertains to your religion.

3. *The Anecdotal Approach*, which considers stories recounting the personal experiences of thousands of persons that have had Near-Death Experiences (NDEs), and After Death Communications

(ADCs) that have been documented in writing over many centuries. There is a huge amount of written material on this subject, and the challenge is to determine the validity of the many amazing personal experiences that are described. Talk about ghost stories!

4. *The Analytical Approach*. This approach can be applied broadly to all of the world's religions - not just the Christian religion. This is the approach that I have taken as an engineer. In Engineering School I was taught how to converge on a solution when I was attempting to solve a problem. This is the approach that I have taken in trying to "prove" that there is an Afterlife.

Figure 1 graphically illustrates how this "solution convergence" process works. If you look at the base of the pyramid, you will note that there are many possible concepts that relate to the problem at hand. For this illustration, these are arbitrarily labeled (1) through (7). When you first start to explore and solve the problem, it can be pretty overwhelming, and this is where the "converging on a solution" technique comes into play.

What you do is to start at the bottom and tackle each aspect of the problem, one at a time. As you solve the smaller individual problems, you reach partial solutions, and you gradually move up from the base of the pyramid. Finally, if you are diligent enough, you reach the top of the pyramid and, low and behold, you have arrived at an overall answer! What this boils down to is that a problem that might seem very imposing at first, gradually gets solved, a step at a time.

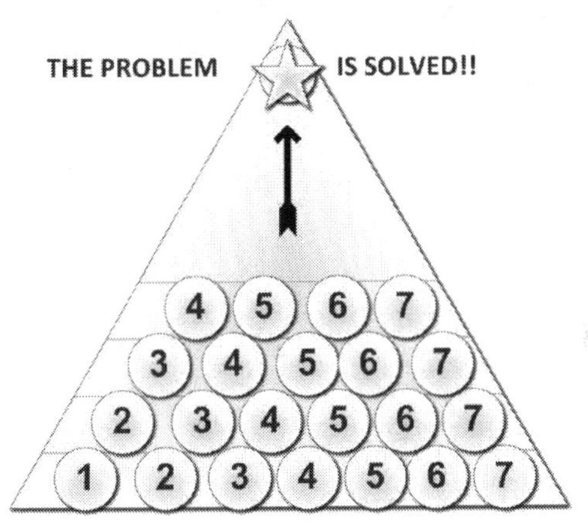

Figure 1- Solution Convergence Pyramid

I find this technique to be very useful. Often in life we face difficult problems, which in some cases may seem insurmountable. But, the upshot of the story is that if you work at the problem methodically, one step at a time, you will eventually reach the top of the pyramid where you will have an answer.

Another way of looking at this would be to have a "Solution Christmas Tree." I kind of like this, because there is always an Angel at the top of the tree. We can always use the help of an Angel when it comes to solving our problem!

Thomas Edison was a great example of using the process of "converging on a solution." When he had the inspiration to develop the incandescent light bulb, he literally tried over 1000 different materials for the filament of the light bulb before he found one that really worked. I once heard a story about Edison, in which someone asked him if he was ever discouraged by his lack of progress when he was searching for a light bulb filament that would work. He said "No" he was making great progress because he now knew of 1000 filaments that did not work!

* * * * * *

All of the different approaches that I have listed above have varying degrees of validity, and each can make a contribution to solving the riddle of how the universe was created, the nature of the true God, and the existence of Spirit World. Perhaps the best way that we can arrive at any sort of "truth" is to look at all of these approaches, and extract elements from each approach that add to our total picture of what life is really all about.

For example, was there really a big bang? This is a theory that is currently accepted by most scientists, but as more data is collected, we may discover that something entirely different created the universe. And, as citizens of the physical world in which we live, what about the Spirit World? When our time in this world is over and we move into that aspect of God's creation (as I believe we do), it is my view that we will have many new insights that are not available to us in the physical world in which we live today.

In attempting to gain perspective on this whole subject, please join me in an imaginative journey back in time – say to the year 1762 – when Mozart was just six years old. At that age, he was entertaining royalty at the Schoenbrunn Palace in Vienna, Austria. He was a true child genius, which only God could create. What a magnificent era that was in terms of the culture of its citizens! Think of the impact his music still has on us today, many centuries later.

Of course, unless you were an upper middle-class citizen, or royalty, you were not able to participate in all of the great cultural aspects of that time. The situation is somewhat different today, in that today nearly everyone in our country, whether rich or poor, has access to radio, television, or recording devices, so they can enjoy cultural events if they are so inclined.

Let's suppose you and I were living in Mozart's era and we were sitting down together in a restaurant drinking tea. Suddenly, I reach into my pocket and pull out a little palm-sized thing, which I then put up to my mouth and start talking into. You wouldn't have a clue as to what was going on, and then when I told you that I was talking to my son that lived in Paris, you would just laugh because you knew that this was totally impossible!

The fact is, in that era we didn't know much about electromagnetic radiation. Yes, we experienced the everyday use of light, but we didn't have a clue about how it worked to enable us to see things, and I'm sure we thought of light as something that was instantaneous, and not as something that traveled at a finite speed of about 186,000 miles per second! Today, we understand most everything about electromagnetic radiation, which covers all of our radio, radar, telephone and satellite communications as well as visible light, ultraviolet light, and infrared light.

But, when it comes to Spirit communication, I feel that we know very little. I think, however, that there is plenty of anecdotal evidence which leads us to believe that it truly exists. I feel that an exploration of the whole field of Spirit communication is a very fertile field for future scientific investigation, and this is very directly connected with our pursuit of a greater understanding of life hereafter.

Chapter 5

My Analytical (Common Sense) Approach

Ever since the dawn of civilization, people have pondered their relationship to a Creator. In ancient times they thought in terms of multiple gods, but today most people acknowledge a single creator or God.

First I would like to state my firm beliefs concerning God and his relationship to man. You may wonder why I decided that these are my firm beliefs. Well, it is my view that they are just common sense. They are not dependent on scientific theory or proof, any belief in the Bible and it's interpretation, belief in the theology of any particular denomination, or any text related to religions other than the Christian religion. They are not related to whether you are a liberal or conservative, or a traditionalist or a progressive. Also, they are not related to the accuracy of any anecdotal evidence.

I appreciate the fact that many people have very strong religious beliefs. For example, some people believe that every word in the Bible is the inspired word of God and is literally true. Then there are other people who call themselves "progressives," who see the stories of the Bible as metaphors and guides for our daily living. I don't believe that my common sense approach will conflict with the views of people in either of these camps. My approach is just a different way of looking at the concept of an Afterlife.

Here are my firm beliefs:

1. There is only one Supreme Being, God, or Intelligent Designer. I can't emphasize this too strongly, because it is basic to my entire belief system. Now when I refer to a Supreme Being or God, I must admit that I know virtually nothing about the nature of God. All I truly believe is that it would be impossible that the universe that we know of could ever have been created without some kind of super-intelligence or God who created our Universe.

2. God is alive today! If He wasn't, all of our prayers would be a waste of time.

3. We can place no limitations on what God can do. Remember, He created our entire universe. Quite a feat! I find it impossible to grasp how this could ever be done, and it may be that it is beyond the capability of the human mind to understand the true nature of creation.

4. There is a communication link, in the Spirit World, that exists between individual human beings and God. One of the ways that man attempts to tap into this link is through what we call "prayer." I believe that this link is always present, although we may not always be conscious of its existence or know how to access it when we wish, or even how to use it effectively.

5. No human being can be completely objective when it comes to considering his relationship to God. We are all products of the environment in which we live, and this affects our individual views of reality.

6. I believe, with 100 % certainty, that it would be impossible to create humankind without the existence of a Supreme Being or "Designer," and I further feel that a skilled theoretical mathematician or physicist may eventually be able to scientifically prove that idea.

7. I believe human beings are God's ultimate creation on this earth, and that they could not be created through a purely random process of evolution. Human beings are amazingly complex, but because we are all human beings we tend to take for granted miracles like breathing, sight, hearing, and the birth of a child. Whether you subscribe to the idea that humans evolved over millions of years, or you believe the story of creation as it is set forth in the book of Genesis, or anything in between, it really makes no difference. The vast universe, the countless creatures of the Earth, and even the miracle of human thought simply had to be directed by a divine creator. He may have created the universe in seven days, or maybe seven days to God is thirteen billion years to us. Either way, it is impossible to watch a bird fly or listen to a Mozart concerto without recognizing the hand of God in the experience.

It seems clear to me that the most astounding creation of all is the human being. Just consider how human beings are created. They start out with the fertilization of a tiny egg by a sperm cell, then over the course of nine months the embryo grows into an extremely complex organism that can eventually walk, talk, sing, and play the piano. We just take it for granted, but this is truly a miracle that has been created by God! Another thing that amazes me is that although all human bodies are very similar, each and every human body has a unique face that is not exactly the same as anyone else's face, and also they have unique fingerprints. This is one way of God saying that every human being is a special one-of-a-kind creation.

Recently I read a book called *One Nation,* written by Dr. Ben Carson, an eminent neurosurgeon. He tells some amazing facts about the human brain, which I have quoted below:

"I can tell you unequivocally that it is impossible to overload the human brain with information. If you learn one new fact every second, which is virtually impossible, it will take you approximately 3,000,000 years to approach brain overload. The human brain has billions of neurons and hundreds of billions of interconnections. It can process more than 2 million bits of information per second and can remember everything you have ever seen or heard.

All of this information is retained indefinitely. I could take an 85-year-old man and place depth electrodes into a certain part of his brain, followed by appropriate electrical stimulation and he would be able to recite back verbatim a book he had read 60 years ago. Most of us can't retrieve the information our brain stores that easily, but surely we can improve."

This is quite a challenge to most of us as we get older, who can't always remember the name of someone we have known for years. Most of us have trouble recalling what we had for breakfast. Just think how compact and sophisticated the human brain is compared to the most sophisticated electronic computers we have produced today!

8. I believe that God truly loves and watches over each of his creations. Now you might wonder how God can keep track of all of the individuals that He has created. At first glance this would seem impossible to do when you consider the billions of people living on this earth. But look at what we have been able to do, as mere mortals, when it comes to technological advancements like the Internet, with the ability to instantly communicate with nearly anyone in the world! Who would have thought, 100 years ago, that it would be possible to do this with a tiny little box that you would hold in your hand.

I believe that if God wishes, He can keep track of everyone, using communication through the Spirit World. We know a lot about electromagnetic transmission, which enables us to enjoy all of our modern wireless communication, but we know very little about communication as it takes place in the Spirit World. Prayer is one way that we believe we can access the Spirit World, but there is great deal we don't know about prayer; why it works in some cases, and appears not to work in other cases.

Some people say that in the Spirit World there are a number of different levels of communication that take place, but we don't really know how to reliably access these levels of communication if, in fact, they do exist. It is difficult for us to truly appreciate the concept of the Spirit World. Nevertheless, there is ample anecdotal evidence that the Spirit World truly exists, and over thousands of years humankind has held remarkably similar beliefs in heaven, and a faith in a life hereafter.

9. Although I firmly believe that it is possible to communicate with God, and with other human beings in the Spirit World, we don't understand the means of communication that makes this possible. There is a great deal of anecdotal evidence that suggests that this happens. Any one incidence of such communication might be open to question, but when you look at the totality of such evidence, there is little doubt that this sort of "extra-sensory" perception does exist.

Now, setting aside for the moment the mystery of our communication with God, let's look at some of the things we do understand with regard to communication.

Today, we live in an increasing wireless world. We can hold that little box in our hand and communicate instantly with almost anyone throughout the entire world. In addition, we can instantly tap into vast storehouses of information contained in the world's libraries and other depositories. Two hundred years ago a person would consider this an absolute miracle, and would have no understanding as to how this was even possible. They might think that this was some sort of magic, or an "act of God."

We now understand the principles of electromagnetic radiation, and have been able to tailor this understanding to create practical devices to use in our everyday lives. We can't directly see, feel, or hear most electromagnetic waves, except for light, but we can use them in practical ways to meet our everyday needs. At home, with a small personal computer, we can access virtually all of the world's knowledge and use it to our advantage in guiding our personal and business lives. This personal computer at home is limited as to what it can do by itself, but the instant it is connected to the Internet, it is able to communicate with an almost unimaginably large consortium of computers on the Internet, which means the possibilities are almost limitless.

I see a parallel between the idea of an isolated computer connecting to the Internet and our connection with God. In today's world, you might say that we have created in the Internet our own mini-god, to facilitate all of our communication needs.

The Creation Of Human Life By God.

As I stated previously, human life is created when a male sperm cell fertilizes a female egg. These two microscopic cells then merge and grow into the exceedingly complex organism known as a human being. It is my belief that in spite of our increasing knowledge of DNA, it is impossible for these two initial cells to truly contain all of the information that is necessary for the creation of a complex human being. If I am correct, then how is it possible to develop a complex human being?

In order to answer this question I am presenting my theory of the relationship of God to humankind.

First, let's look at an analogy between things that we know about, and things that we still do not fully understand. Earlier, I talked about the relationship between a personal computer terminal and a large number of distributed computers, and how the connection between the two entities gives tremendous power to the capabilities of that personal computer.

Now let's think of God as an infinitely large storehouse of information. A vast Cosmic Internet, so to speak, that can keep track of every form of life that has ever been created. It is beyond the capacity of the human mind to fully understand the infinite capabilities of the "mind" of our Creator. I firmly believe, also, that we can place no limits on the abilities of God in relation to the design of the universe and all its inhabitants. When it comes to the creation of human life on this earth, I believe that, from the moment of conception, the human "soul" is in constant communication with God, and this is what truly enables the cells, as they grow and multiply, to create an exceedingly complex human being.

Birth today is so commonplace, that we forget that it is a great miracle! Consider the human brain, far more complex than our most sophisticated computers. And there is self-awareness of existence in each of us that is not present in any computer that we have created. In my view, I doubt that we will ever be able to create a computer that is truly self-aware. This appears to be only something that God can create.

We really don't know exactly what the medium of communication is between God and ourselves, but there is very strong evidence it does exist, and that it is vital to our existence in this world today. We've been able to measure radio waves, light waves, and sound waves, but as of today we have not been able to measure any sort of "Spirit waves" that would enable us to communicate with God. In fact, they may not even be waves. This is a great mystery to us, and it may be that we will never be able to fully understand exactly how this takes place. Prayer does seem to connect us with God in many instances, though, and maybe this is all we will ever need to know.

At this point, I realize that some of my readers may disagree with some of my assumptions. If so, I would welcome your frank comments in this regard. I would also welcome the comments of mathematicians, theoretical scientists, and any others who may feel they are in a position to "prove" (or disprove) some of my assumptions. I am still on my faith journey, and am continuing to get new insights as to what life is all about. I believe that through frank interaction with other people, we can all grow in understanding as we travel on our individual faith journeys.

Even though what I have presented purports to be a new theory, I in no way want to infer that a religion based solely on faith is not adequate for many people. The Bible still gives Christians the most solid evidence of our religious heritage, and fills many persons' needs for a solid relationship with God. This book is written from the perspective of a person brought up in the traditional Christian faith, but I believe that much of what I have proposed is valid for most all of the world's great religions.

More on this later in Chapter 9.

Chapter 6

Coincidence Or Divine Intervention?

As I look back over the 94 years of my life, I realize that many things happened that I originally thought were merely coincidences. In my younger years it never occurred to me that many of these things might have been caused by the impact of God on my life. Frankly, in those days, I was not thinking a lot about God, as I was spending most of my time earning a living, and my wife and I were busy bringing up a wonderful family of four children. We were simply too busy to wonder about such things.

But now, given the perspective of time, I really feel that God has always had a much stronger influence on my life than I realized; I suppose I would say this is now just my "common sense" view.

Earlier in this book you read a brief résumé of my working experience. As you know, after I went into the motion picture business I had a number of fortunate things happen that I thought of as just coincidences. But now, I realize that it was extremely unlikely that these were merely due to chance.

First, I would like to talk about the movie that we made for Orme School in Arizona. When we were first contacted by Orme School, we had only made one movie, a simple film just to get some experience in producing a professional 16mm sound film with dialogue and music. Prior to that, my only experience was in shooting home movies.

Somehow or other we managed to get an order from Orme School to produce a promotional film for them – hard to believe, since they had never seen anything we had produced. Would you buy a product from a brand-new company without ever seeing a sample of their product? I certainly wouldn't. But we were able to convince them that we could do the job, so they gave it to us. Was this just a coincidence? I doubt it.

After we got the order, they told me that Jimmy Stewart was an honorary trustee of the school, and perhaps he would agree to be in the film. They asked him, and his answer, amazingly, was "Yes." Wow! Jimmy Stewart was my very favorite Hollywood actor, and I could hardly believe that I was going to be directing him in a film. Please keep in mind that I had never directed anything before in my life!

The next component in a successful film is an excellent script. Our first script was written by a lady from Colorado, but somehow she did not seem to know how to write an effective script that would work for Jimmy Stewart. We had her do a rewrite, and it still didn't work. Then we just "happened" to be contacted by a man named Bruce Henry, a retired screen writer who had just moved to Arizona. He saw our name in the telephone book and thought we might have some interest in having him write some scripts for us. Bruce took a shot at writing the script for the Orme School film, and he did a superb job. Somehow he knew how to write words that sounded like they were coming directly from Jimmy Stewart's heart.

So I did direct Jimmy Stewart, and the film was a resounding success. It won many awards, and the film, now converted to video, is still being used today to promote Orme School. When you hear about all the things that came together to make that film happen, you might say, "Well, all that was just a series of fortunate coincidences!" Looking back, even I have no idea where I got the skills and courage to tackle this job, but I truly believe that entire episode in my life was a gift directly from God.

Years later, I was privileged to become the Scoutmaster of Boy Scout Troop #4 in Scottsdale, Arizona. As a new Scoutmaster, I was looking for ways to attract more adults to the Troop Committee, so I checked with the National Headquarters of Boy Scouts to see if they had any films that I could use for this purpose. They did have a film, but it was so obsolete that I did not want to use it.

So I decided that perhaps I could make a film for this purpose. Fortunately, I was able to secure some money from the local Boy Scout Council in Phoenix to enable me to make this film. I could do it very inexpensively for them because I could shoot much of the film while I was on camping trips with my own Scout troop.

After I secured the contract to produce the film, someone said Dick Van Dyke is living in Carefree, Arizona, and maybe he would be willing to appear in the film. He was asked about this, and he said "Yes." Here we go again - I had another opportunity to deal with a celebrity. At that time, Dick Van Dyke was very popular, and he was always one of the movie stars whose work I really enjoyed. I spent a day shooting our film with him and a Boy Scout troop in the Superstition Mountain area of Arizona. Again, we were very successful and we won a Freedoms Foundation award for this film. Once again, I see the hand of God in making all this happen.

So far, I've been talking about events from many years ago. Now, I would like to tell you about a situation that happened about a year ago which I truly believe is a lot more than just a coincidence.

In preparation for the book you're reading right now, I had been doing a great deal of research concerning book writing and promotion. During this research I came across the name of a man named Scott Lorenz, who is a specialist in book marketing and public relations. When I wrote to him, I told him a little bit about my background, and I briefly mentioned that my company, Swartwout Productions, produced a TV commercial that won an award in the Guinness Book of World Records as the longest running TV commercial in the world. This was a commercial called "Thank You," produced for the Discount Tire Company, featuring a little old lady who returns a tire to them by throwing it through one of their large plate glass windows!

It turns out that the very day that Scott received my letter, a client of his walked in to his office and said to him that he would like to produce a TV commercial that was as simple and effective as that Discount Tire ad with the little old lady in it.

The chances of this just being a coincidence are miniscule, and I am confident that this had to be divine intervention. The "magic" continues! I'm sure that God works in wonderful ways that we do not understand, but it is my firm belief that as time goes on and as further research continues, we can learn a great deal more about how this all happens. As you will note in later chapters, I am pushing for a major program of scientific research to tell us more about the Afterlife and how communication works in the Spirit World. If all this really does come to pass, it will be because of God's continuing help.

Chapter 7

A Well-Done "Medium" Is Rare

Up to this point, our discussion has been pretty serious, but I just couldn't resist that chapter title. I certainly don't mean to be disrespectful toward people who communicate with the Spirit World, often called "mediums." This has been one of the most difficult chapters to write, because there are many people who profess to be mediums who are actually fakes.

After my wife died, I was desperate to learn more about the Afterlife. Because of my early religious training, I believed in the Afterlife, but I wanted more proof. As I read about the Afterlife and the idea of mediums, I became academically convinced that it was possible, working with a true medium, to communicate with persons in the Spirit World. There is a great deal of anecdotal information in books I have read detailing the experiences people have had while working with mediums, and some of their stories are quite amazing.

By the way, I looked up the meaning of the word "anecdotal" on the internet and here is what I found:

an·ec·do·tal /adjective (of an account) not necessarily true or reliable, because based on personal accounts rather than facts or research.

People like to share stories about things that happened to them, or that they heard about, to make a point. This kind of talk is anecdotal, based on personal accounts. Anecdotal stories are helpful when you're trying to convey an example of something, but there's a downside to anecdotal information; since it's not necessarily based on facts, you never know if you can totally trust it. So it's best to go beyond the anecdotal and get more solid information, and that is the goal of my book.

What this says to me is that I must be very careful if I use anecdotal evidence to try and prove a point. I may be able to rely on this kind of evidence only if there is an overwhelming amount of evidence that tends to prove the point I am trying to make.

I also realize that it is an established fact that there are a lot of "fakers" who purport to be genuine mediums, but are not really in touch with the Spirit World. These people are often called "cold readers." These "cold readers" have learned techniques to subtly extract information from you without you realizing what they are doing, so that you believe that the information is coming from a contact they have with the Spirit World.

The problem that you face, if you wish to try to work with a medium, is to determine that the person you are working with is genuine, and not a fake. There are excellent lists on the Internet of so-called "approved mediums." If you plan to work with a medium, it pays to contact someone on one of these "approved" lists. Or as an alternative, if you have a personal friend who has had a great experience with a medium, this can be another source for finding one who is really bona fide.

Before getting into my personal experience with some mediums, I would like to back up and give you a little history about mediums and psychics. From what I have read, ever since humankind appeared on this earth, there has been an interest in the Spirit World, and about learning what happens to our souls after we die.

During the last part of the 19th century in England, there was a lot of activity dealing with the Spirit World. There were mediums, palm readers, tea leaf readers, psychics, séance leaders, Ouija boards, and many other paths to the Spirit World. There were even some prestigious British organizations that were scientifically examining all aspects of communication with the Spirit World.

During the 20th century, there was an increasing amount of this kind of activity in the United States. I think that at first, many persons felt there was something "strange" about you if you believed in these things. But as time went on, there has been greater acceptance of some of this thinking, and today I feel like there is a great deal of interest and greater acceptance of the idea of exploring the Spirit World. Almost everyone I talk to about the book I am writing expresses a great deal of interest in the Afterlife.

When I was a young man I was very impressed with the explorations being made by Dr. Rhine at Duke University. He did a lot of work with specialized playing cards to prove that the mind was capable of sensing some things that were not obvious. He had made up some cards with special symbols on them, and then he would have two people sit in separate rooms. As one person turned down each card in his deck, the person in the other room would try to guess which card was turned down. Well, if this was purely a random situation, they would only be right about 50% of the time. However, with many of his subjects he found that they had scores that were much higher than 50%, which indicated there was some kind of mental telepathy involved.

Today, I don't believe we really understand how mental telepathy works, but I think it is a well-established fact that true mental telepathy exists, and I feel it is somehow or other related to the world of Spirit communication.

Even though there has been quite a lot of scientific exploration going on, the idea of communicating with the Spirit World was, and still is, often used as entertainment. I remember one instance in which, many years ago, my parents went to a party where the hostess had hired a tea-leaf reader to entertain the group. When my dad told me about the experience, he was very surprised and impressed, because she told him he was having a management problem with a key employee at his company. She described this employee's appearance very accurately, as he had an unusual haircut, which really impressed my dad. He knew that it was impossible that she would have any way of knowing about this specific situation – or that haircut.

More recently, I attended a program in Sedona at our Performing Arts Center where a well-known magician by the name of Kreskin performed. The bulk of the performance consisted of what you might call traditional magic tricks, but at the end of his performance, he held a séance. He invited about 40 people at random from the audience, to the stage and they were seated in groups of four around 10 card tables. They placed their hands flat on the tops of the card tables, and you could clearly see underneath all the tables that their knees were not in any contact with the undersides of the tables. Kreskin was able to get these tables to move all around on the stage, and it was very obvious that the persons sitting at the tables could not make this happen. As far as I was concerned, what I observed was a genuine séance. I don't have any idea how he could have been able to make this happen, and it did not seem like this was just some sort of explainable magic trick. It appeared to all of us that these tables were actually controlled by Kreskin's mind. Still, throughout his career and to this very day, Kreskin has denied being a real psychic or medium, and claims that everything he does is an illusion that relies on the power of suggestion.

Wow! There is a lot we don't know about how the mind works.

Still, I believe that it has been well established that after a person dies, the mind of this person still exists, and continues to live on in the Spirit World. Some of us may think of this as the human soul. I was very eager to have contact with the soul of my deceased wife, so I decided to try and contact her through a medium who was on one of the lists of so-called legitimate mediums.

When a medium makes a significant contact it is called a "hit." These legitimate mediums don't claim to be able to make 100% hits with the person with whom you would like to connect, but it appears that the better ones can make hits about 80% of the time.

I was eagerly looking forward to this first session with a medium, but it turned out to be a great disappointment. After about 5 to 10 minutes it was obvious that we were getting nowhere, so the medium suggested that we cancel the session and that my money would be refunded. Even though this first session was very disappointing, I still was a strong believer in mediums, based on what I read and what I had heard from a personal friend who had some great experiences.

I contacted another medium who had been highly recommended to me. Again, it was not a very successful session, and the medium agreed to refund a substantial portion of the fee that had been charged. By this time I had started writing my book about the Afterlife, and I felt that I still wanted to have a successful sitting with a medium, because I felt that this was the only way I could become a "knowing" person.

I went on to work with a couple of additional mediums, but again no real success from what I felt was my objective viewpoint. At this point I was feeling quite discouraged, as I expected that, perhaps, the only thing that would convert me from being a believer to a "knowing" person was to be able to have a successful contact with my wife with help from a legitimate medium.

After further reading on the subject of mediums, I learned that when effective contact with loved ones that had passed over could not be established, that sometimes the problem was with the sitter and not with the medium. This surprised me, but the more I thought about it I realized that even though I believed in the reality of mediums, I was a person who found it very difficult to meditate, and perhaps this was part of the problem. I have a very active mind, and it was hard for me to get rid of the daily clutter of everything that was going on.

As time went on and I was nearing the completion of the first draft of my book, I decided to take one more shot at reaching into the Spirit World with a medium. I contacted a good friend who gave me the name of another medium, Susanne Wilson, and he suggested that I contact her. I did, and this time I hit the jackpot! This was a one hour session, and in the paragraphs below I will summarize some of the high points of the sitting I had with her.

She started with an opening prayer, and after that she was surprised to find herself overwhelmed with a large number of people from the Spirit World who were trying to get in contact with me, working through her. In the early part of our session, she came up with my wife's name, Gretchen.

This is a rather unusual name, and this is the first time in any of my sessions where my wife's name had been identified. She also came up with the name of one of my sons. Further, she learned from her contact with the Spirit World that both my wife and I were very creative. She was able to tell me that my wife, Gretchen, was a painter, and that I had been involved in motion pictures and art. Susanne said that my wife thanked me for giving an annual cash award, in her honor, at the Spring Show of the Northern Arizona Watercolor Association, a thing that I have done every year since Gretchen died.

She did mention a few names that I could not identify, but overall I would give her an accuracy rating of about 80%, which I consider to be very good.

Recently I had another session with Susanne Wilson, and it was also very successful. She told me a number of things that astounded me. I told Susanne that I was writing a book, but I made no mention of the cover of the book in my comments to Susanne. When she communicated with Gretchen, she learned that Gretchen knew that I was planning to use a copy of one of her watercolor paintings on the front cover of the book. Gretchen encouraged me to do this, and also wanted me to make sure that the color of the original painting was faithfully reproduced. As I had not previously given any information to Susanne about the book cover, the only way she could have known about this was if she had received the information from Gretchen! This just further solidified my belief that I was now a "knowing" person concerning the reality of a medium being able to communicate with persons in the Spirit World.

There is one frustration, however, in my experience when working with Susanne; it appears that the control of the "session" is by the person or persons in the Spirit World and is not in the hands of the medium, meaning that the medium cannot guarantee that they will be able to get in touch with a specific person.

I would like to emphasize the point that you should not let yourself be discouraged if your first contact with a medium is non-productive. Based on my experience, it pays to have a little bit of patience, and work with several different mediums before coming to the conclusion that this is not a valid way of contacting your loved one that has departed to the Spirit World. It is my belief that you will eventually find a medium that can truly establish a connection with your loved ones.

Chapter 8

Near-Death Experiences (NDE) & After-Death Communication (ADC)

There are many amazing stories about NDEs, but as you read about them, please remember that these people did not die; they had only been near death.

In the written literature, there is documentation covering hundreds if not thousands of near death experiences. A substantial number of these experiences are similar, in that the person involved seemed to see a long dark tunnel, and at the end of the long tunnel there was a very bright light. In some cases it appears that the person was given the option of continuing on through the tunnel to the bright light area, or going back to their life on this earth. Although there was a lot of similarity in many of the stories, there were also a lot of differences. In my conservative analysis, I need to put all of these NDEs into the anecdotal category.

Also, there are many accounts of experiences

where living persons have received communications directly from persons who have died. These experiences are categorized as After Death Communication (ADC). Some of these images appear to be ethereal (more ghost-like), but also many have been images of people who appear to be solid three-dimensional apparitions. Also, many of these experiences seem to be well-documented. What this says to me is that while any one instance might be open to question, there is little doubt in my mind that there is validity to many of these situations that have been reported.

I will not attempt to document all of the recorded cases of NDEs and ADCs that have been reported, and continue to be reported on a regular basis. In my bibliography at the end of this book, there are a number of book titles listed that will give you a great deal of additional information.

I would like to call your attention to one book in particular that has been a milestone in regard to (NDEs) This book was written by Dr., Raymond A. Moody, Jr., M.D. and was originally published in 1975, and has sold over 13 million copies around the globe!

Chapter 9

Our Quest for Greater Knowledge of the Universe

Ever since the dawn of civilization, I feel that people must have been awed as they looked up at the skies at the tremendous display of stars. I sense that they must have wondered how they could possibly relate to this overwhelming display. Today, we are very much involved in exploring the universe in an attempt to learn more about how it came about, and how we fit into this entire picture.

Today we are spending billions of dollars in order to learn about our universe and our role in it. The first big feat was our landing of men on the moon, an amazing accomplishment. The US has already landed a vehicle on Mars, and a program is underway in which we plan to actually send people to Mars. I understand that over 1000 brave souls have volunteered to go on a one-way trip to Mars, but I doubt that we will ever embark on a project in which we do not plan to bring our astronauts back to the earth.

Just recently we are starting to receive some amazing photographs of the planet Pluto. It takes 4.6 hours for the radio waves to travel the 4.6 billion miles to Earth from the space vehicle that is photographing Pluto!

Also, the United States is participating in a large project in South America called the "Atacama Large Millimeter Array." This is an astronomical interferometer of radio telescopes in the Atacama desert of northern Chile. This is located on a plateau at an altitude of 16,500 feet. It consists of 66 23-foot diameter radio telescopes receiving at millimeter and sub-millimeter wavelengths, and has been operational since March 2013. This year they are linking the Atacama telescope with radio telescopes in Antarctica, Mexico, and Hawaii to form a planet-sized "virtual telescope" powerful enough to study the black hole at the center of the Milky Way. You can't actually see a black hole, since the immense gravity literally swallows light, but they hope to gather data about the edge, called the "event horizon."

We were motivated to do all this by our insatiable quest to learn about possible life on other planets throughout the universe. It is inconceivable that we are the only planet in the universe that has life on it, but I don't believe we have as yet made contact with any other planetary life. I realize that some people claim to have made contact with beings from other planets, but this appears to be anecdotal evidence which is very controversial.

One problem is that all of the information we receive today comes to us at the speed of light, and when you relate this speed to the size of our universe, that speed is incredibly slow. It can take billions of years for us to receive any information from the far reaches of our universe.

Until recently, we thought that this was the fastest that any information could travel in our universe, but in recent years we have discovered a new phenomenon called "quantum entanglement." What we have determined is that two photons that were generated together and then separated by a vast distance will maintain virtually instantaneous communication with each other. It is significant that a change that is made in one photon will immediately appear in the other photon, no matter how great the distance between the two particles. This "quantum entanglement" phenomenon cannot, as yet, be completely explained by any accepted theory, but it may mean that the speed of light is no longer a limitation.

One theory that has been proposed suggests that all particles in the universe were once tightly compacted and, as a result still maintain a connectedness. Of course, this seems to presuppose that the "big bang" theory is a reality, but this has not been proven as yet. Even though there is not a generally accepted theory of Entanglement, the observation that it occurs has been scientifically verified. To my mind this means that "it's a whole new ballgame," and I believe it just might open the door to a new era of exploration, as we seek to learn more of the secrets of our universe.

Chapter 10

Religions Other Than Christianity

The Pew Research Center has recently published a very comprehensive report on the future of world religions, as related to population growth projections from 2010 to 2050. Listed below are some of the highlights of this report:

Relative Size and Projected Growth of Major Religious Groups

Christians	*2,168,330,000*
2050 (projected)	*2,918,070,000*
Muslims	*1,599,700,000*
2050 (projected)	*2,761,480,000*
Unaffiliated	*1,131,150,000*
2050 (projected)	*1,230,340,000*
Hindus	*1,032,210,000*
2050 (projected)	*1,384,360,000*

Buddhists	*487,760,000*
2050 (projected)	*486,270,000*
Folk Religions	*404,690,000*
2050 (projected)	*449,140,000*
Jews	*13,860,000*
2050 (projected)	*16,090,000*
Other Religions	*58,150,000*
2050 (projected)	*61,450,000*
World total	*6,895,850,000*
2050 (projected)	*9,307,190,000*

When you look at the above chart, it is apparent that in 2010 the Christian religion was, by far the largest religious group in the world, and this is still true today in 2015. When you look at the projected 2050 population, the Christian religion is still the biggest population, but the Muslim religion will have grown to where it is running a very close second to the Christians. If this trend continues, it won't be very long before the Muslims will outnumber Christians in the world. I don't personally understand why the Muslim population is growing so rapidly, but circumstances could change, which would alter the projected 2050 populations. Only time will tell.

It is a known fact that today most all of the so-called main-line Protestant denominations are declining in attendance. There are a lot of people today who say they are "religious," but they are not affiliated with any particular denomination. Also, many young persons feel that religion is not pertinent to their lives.

It is beyond the scope of this book to go into detailed information about all of the world's religions, but I believe that there are many good things that the world's religions have in common. If we could just learn to work together concerning our common interests, I feel that it would become apparent to most every person in the world that we all have the same desires in life.

As I am writing this, I just received a letter from my granddaughter, Roxanne Stehlik, who is currently spending two years with the Peace Corps in Peru. Quoted below are her comments which I feel beautifully express how all persons are the same in many ways. So why are we always fighting each other?

"The longer I wander, and the more that I see, the more that I am overwhelmed not by the differences in the world, but by the multitude of ways that we are all the same. Of course, culture is the name we give to the robe that we wrap ourselves in, and the one we dress our children in and pass on to our grandchildren. But beneath the bright and varied colors, so much is the same. Here, we dance cumbia. We dance festejo, and we dance marinera. We listen

to huayno and hear stories told in quechua. Where I am from, we dance waltzes, or swing. But still we dance. We all dance.

Here we wash our clothes by hand, standing in the sunshine, pounding out the dirt on the banks of a river or in the sink on rooftop. There, we use a washing machine. But still, we wash our clothes. Here weddings can last for days. The party goes on and on as the bride and groom host luncheons, dances, and carry their wedding cake around town, delivering pieces to the invited guests. There, our weddings are briefer. But people still marry. They still celebrate.

I walk to the beach and see children playing in the sand, burying themselves, and I remember years ago, on the other side of the globe, doing just the same thing as I reveled in the sand between my toes. My host family cries. When they are hurt, they weep for the pain that someone caused them. They have problems. Not everyone gets along. Just like where I come from. Traveling is a beautiful experience. There is something magical in seeing people all over the world as they display their personalities and their values in a brilliant display of differences.

But the longer I wander, the more I realize that we really aren't very different. People seek out love. People hunger for knowledge. They want to feel needed and valued. Children yearn for the approval and attention of their parents, and parents wonder what will happen to their children, worrying over the millions of things they cannot control. People slip through the cracks. It happens everywhere. Loneliness exists in big cities and small towns, in the mountains, and on the beach. And happiness is found amongst the barefooted, perhaps even more often than it is found amongst those with a closet full of shoes. There are countless similarities between people no matter where I go.

The longer I stay and the more I take time to understand those around me, the more I realize that the behaviors that at first seem strange, are just a different way to try and obtain the same goal that I recognize everywhere. I may believe I'm walking right side up and someone else is walking sideways on the face of the earth, but it turns out that the way we're walking has more to do with where we're watching from than where our feet are.

Deep down, we're rooted in so many of the same realities. And yet, despite that, innumerable differences in the way we play out those realities so often mask the similarities beneath. And the beauty of traveling, of living with others is the opportunity to revel not only in the similarities, but in the differences as well."

Now that we have instantaneous, world-wide, communication with almost everyone, it is my hope that this will be helpful in reducing the tensions between the various religions, but so far, this has not been the case. I believe that all human beings were created by one God, who loves each of us. It is also my belief that nearly all the conflicts between different religions have been created by men who have not always used their God-given intellects in the best way. I believe that once we understand more about the Spirt World, it will be helpful in creating harmony among all the people on this earth.

More about this in Appendix 1, where I will present my dream for eliminating World Wars in the future.

Chapter 11

The Channel of the Future – The Spirit World

I originally planned to call this chapter, "The Wave of the Future," but then I realized that I really didn't know if communication in the Spirit World is by any sort of "wave," so I decided to use the word "Channel." Waves are the medium we currently use to do most all of our communicating today. When we talk to each other we are using sound waves in the air that surrounds us. When we tune in to the radio or TV, or use our cell phones, we are using electromagnetic waves. And when we read a book, or look around and see the beautiful world that God has created, we are using light waves. In other words, most all of our communication that we have both visually and audibly is through various kinds of waves.

I believe that the Spirit World is another huge realm of communication that may or may not be a "wave." Now, I have no idea at this point how Spirit communication actually works, and to the best of my knowledge no person living on this earth really does, but I believe there is very strong anecdotal evidence that this kind of communication really does exist. In addition, there is some experimental work being done, in a rigorous manner, that tends to prove that there is a Spirit World, and that some people are able to regularly communicate with it. At the present time, this communication is far from 100% reliable, but I believe that there is a significant amount of Spirit communication taking place today that would fit into the category of being about 80% reliable.

We know that electromagnetic communication takes place at the speed of light, roughly 186,000 miles per second. This seems to be very fast, but when you look at the idea of communicating with other worlds that may exist in our universe many light years away, this speed is indeed extremely slow. This is just a guess, as I have nothing except "common sense" to support it, but I believe that communication with the Spirit World may be virtually instantaneous. If this is correct, it would be theoretically possible to communicate with other civilizations, which could be located thousands, or even millions of light years away. At this point, I am not aware that anyone has conducted scientific research that would tell us if this is truly the case.

We have spent a considerable amount of money trying to detect possible radio signals that might be coming toward us from other planets. As I mentioned previously, huge dishes are aimed at outer space, but so far we have detected nothing that we can say comes from any type of intelligent source in outer space. Of course, all of our research to date is only trying to pick up radio waves, and we know that they travel at a relatively slow speed with relation to the size of the universe. From my perspective, this just further emphasizes the need for research into the area of Spirit communication. As I briefly discussed earlier, the "entanglement theory" appears to prove that there can be instantaneous communication between two photons that were initially together and then separated at a distance.

There is a great deal that we really don't understand, but when you look back at all of the scientific progress that has been made in the last 100 years, just think about all of the new things we may learn in the next few centuries. Frankly, it blows my mind when I think about this, and I'm sure I can't even begin to imagine some of the breakthroughs that mankind will make in the not too distant future.

Now, if you accept the statement that I made in the title of this book, that *You Don't Die – You Just Change Channels*, then I believe that all of us will be aware, once we are in the Spirit World, of many things that will be taking place in our future, that we cannot understand or even imagine today.

When we change channels on the TV, it is easy to do because we are working in just one medium of transmission – electromagnetic waves. When we change channels into the Spirit World, however, it is a very different situation, as I believe we are changing to a different medium of transmission – Spirit transmission- which we know practically nothing about. I think that when we have a greater understanding of how Spirit communication works, it will begin to open up the mystery of the universe in which we live. I see this as our challenge for future exploration.

Chapter 12
Far-Out Concepts

Before writing on this subject, I would like to set the stage; let's talk a little bit about infinity.

From my perspective, I think it is probably impossible for any human being to truly grasp the physical concept of infinity. I think that mathematicians may have the best understanding of what this means, at least from the framework of mathematics. When I think of infinity, I think of its application to both space and time. The question then arises, what is there beyond infinity? Well, I guess the answer would be nothing, but I find it impossible to grasp this total picture. Perhaps the feedback from some of my readers will give me greater insight to this.

We don't know for sure how large the universe is, but if it is infinitely large, that means that it goes on forever. What this says to me is that it is possible that there could be millions, if not billions, of other "Earths" that exists in the universe.

It is logical, perhaps, to assume that some of these other planets would be populated by people similar to us, but we don't know if this is the case. So far, I have not seen any solid evidence that we have been contacted by persons from planets other than our own.

These other worlds could be very different! Do any of them have the equivalent of a Grand Canyon? Or a Sedona? Or a Mt. Everest? It is unlikely that anything identical to this exists on other planets, but I would presume that they have their own attractions that are unique. To get the answers to these questions, perhaps all we have to do is die! Or, should I say, Change Channels?

I am hopeful, however, that with a great deal of further scientific research into the nature of the spiritual world, we will be able to learn how to spiritually transport ourselves to some of these other "Earths." I am assuming that in the Spirit World there is instantaneous transmission, and we are not limited by the speed of light. This brings up the idea of teleportation. Again, there are people who claim that this exists today, and this is discussed in some of the books that I have read, listed in the bibliography at the end of this book.

In doing my research for this book I've read a number of books that deal with encounters people on this planet claim to have had with flying saucers and their inhabitants. These purport to be all true stories, but I have not been able to verify their validity. Again, feedback from my readers may be helpful in this regard.

I know that some people feel that there is a lot of information about flying saucers that purports to be part of some sort of secret government project or cover-up. It's hard for me to believe this could be the case, however, because we do not seem to be very good at keeping government secrets! Eventually, the "truth" about these projects would become known to the general public.

Another very interesting subject is "time travel." Again, there are books that claim that this is possible and that it is happening today. I know that as human beings on this earth, most of us believe that it is not possible to be able to travel back and forth in time. Time is often considered to be the so-called "fifth dimension" and there are some persons who claim to be able to move back and forth in this dimension while they are still living human beings on our earth. If this is possible, then we could learn a great deal by going back to when Jesus was living on our earth. It would seem to me that this would be extremely helpful to those people who are researching the accuracy of the Bible. At this point, I am not aware of anyone who claims to have travelled back to the time when Jesus was living.

Another subject that relates to our lives on this earth is what happens after we die? As you know, from the title of this book, I believe that we "change channels" and in that sense, we don't die – our souls merely revert back to the Spirit World where it appears we may have been in existence before we were born on this earth. This situation is complicated, however, and is very different than changing channels on your TV. When you do this on TV, you are still working in the same medium of electromagnetic wave transmission regardless of which channel you are accessing. When we die, however, we are then "living" in the Spirit World which is a means of communication we really know very little about. This is where I believe we need to do a great deal of scientific research in the future.

There have been a number of documented cases in which people have appeared to be clinically dead, and were then resuscitated and brought back to life. Some of these people have told amazing stories about the "Afterlife," but please be aware that these people were never really dead – they had only had Near Death Experiences (NDEs). These NDEs do, however, purport to give us insights into what we will enjoy when we are in heaven.

In doing my research for this book, I have just scratched the surface of all of the available literature dealing with the Afterlife. This is why I am looking forward to the feedback that I hope to receive from many of you who have read this book. I believe that the knowledge that I will receive from your feedback will add a great deal of meaningful understanding to the riddle of the Afterlife, and, hopefully, this can form the basis of a second book in which I can share these ideas with everyone.

Chapter 13

A New Beginning (This Is Not the End)

I believe some of the greatest advances that will be made in the future will come from co-operative research between religion and science. Today, many people get all hung up by the so-called "separation of church and state" doctrine, but we must be careful not to misinterpret this concept. It is simply something instituted in the Constitution by our Founding Fathers to prevent our country from falling into the kind of despotic theocracies they had escaped by leaving Europe. It in no way should interfere with in-depth exploration of the role of science in learning more about the Spirit World.

There is some interesting work going on today throughout the country in which people are beginning to combine the concepts of science and religion in order to see more clearly the future of the human spirit in our world. Yes, there may be areas of disagreement between "organized religion," and science, but in my view, organized religion is man-made. Organized religion started with myths and fables, and over the centuries has been used to "control the masses." Sometimes this control may have benefited the people, but all too often it was primarily used for the political benefit of those in charge.

As I write this on what is Father's Day in the USA, I can't help but think of our "Father" in heaven. We don't know much about God, but I think that ever since the dawn of humankind there has been a yearning for a closeness to our Creator. This is very natural, just as it is natural for us to yearn for closeness to our father and mother in this world.

By now, I think you all must realize that I am a dreamer. I firmly believe, however, that before you can accomplish something exciting you must have a dream or vision, and then with hard work you may be able to change the vision into reality.

Back in Chapter 4, you joined me on an imaginary trip in time in which we went back to Vienna, Austria in the 1700s. This was relatively easy for us to do, because we have a lot of documented historical information about what life in Vienna was like in the 1700s. Now, I would like to have you join me on an imaginary trip 500 to 1000 years into the future! This is more difficult because no one, living today (to the best of my knowledge) has ever been there. Before we attempt to look 500 years into the future, however, let's first look just 20 or 30 years in the future. Since this is relatively close to where we are today I believe that I may be able to predict with some degree of accuracy what some aspects of life will be like at that time. Many of you living today will live long enough to find out if my predictions were accurate.

I'm pretty sure that I will also know, but I will be viewing the situation from a very different vantage point!

I think the biggest advances will be made in the area of communications. In our homes we may have a room where one entire wall of the room from floor to ceiling will be a huge super high-definition video screen. This video screen will be in three dimensions, and people who appear on the screen will look so lifelike that you will find it difficult to tell that they are not really physically there, even though they may actually be thousands of miles away in another city. What this means is that in many cases we won't need to take that long trip to meet with other people. We will just be able to invite them into our living room via our living "3-D TeleRoom." If you wish to visit the Grand Canyon, you would be able to do this while seated comfortably in your living room at home.

You might say this is great, but I'm not so sure. I have taken several trips in which I've hiked to the bottom of the Grand Canyon, and I don't think my living room screen could in any way provide the same kind of experience I had scrambling over those rocks. And, I would hate to miss the opportunity to hug my grandson when I see him on that screen.

This does mean however, that many personal and business trips could be eliminated with our virtual reality video experience. This could ultimately result in the saving of many miles of highway and airplane travel – and make it possible for us to arrange to stay closer to those grandkids!

At my age, the odds are pretty good that I won't be living long enough on this earth to see if my prediction is correct, but never fear. I do expect to be monitoring everything happening in this world from my vantage point in the Spirit World! And just maybe, by then I will also be able to talk personally with you from my personal easy chair in Heaven. Wouldn't that be a great, life-changing, experience?

Well, now let's go ahead and take that 500 year look ahead into the future. Of course, this scenario is just a guess on my part, but I would like to think that it is an educated guess; only time will tell. Again, let's suppose the two of us are sitting down at a table having coffee, and I started talking to you about how difficult it used to be in the "olden days" to get from here to there. "Just think," I might say, "I understand that if you wanted to go from Los Angeles to New York City you had to go to what they called an 'airport' and stand in long lines before you had to shuffle into this long silver tube, where you would then have to sit cooped-up for hours on end with dozens of other people. You would eventually arrive in New York City (unless the weather was bad!). Well, here in the year 2516 it is so much easier to just walk into the tele-transporter and get disassembled, then reassembled in New York City in just a few milliseconds!"

Now all of this may seem impossible, but remember how unreal it seemed for us to be able to sit in Vienna and talk to a friend in Paris when we were on our imaginary trip to the 1700s. Also, consider the huge amount of scientific progress we have made in the last 50 to 100 years. Prior to that, there was no such thing as an electronic computer, cell phone, television, etc. I don't think today's kids can even imagine what life was like before there were computers, cell phones, social media, and all the other technology they take for granted.

What would they do if they didn't have text messaging?

We are all very much accustomed to the world around us, right here and now. This is all we really know, so it seems very natural. If we were living back in the days of the cave dwellers, we might have been pretty good at making drawings of the animals on the walls. At that time human civilization had not advanced to the point where we knew how to build housing, so to deal with the rain and the cold, we would have sought out an area where we could find caves to protect us from the elements. This would have been the only world we knew, and so it would have seemed totally normal to us.

What I am trying to say is that it is very difficult, or even impossible, for us to get into the mind-set of someone living on this earth 500 or more years from now. At this point all we are doing is just guessing, and I'm the first to admit that your guess is as good as mine – maybe even better! I will be interested in your feedback on this subject.

However, if we can eventually learn how Spirit communication works, we might open up all kinds of insights into the future. We might be able to travel or at least see into the future or the past. Maybe we could communicate or travel instantly across any distance. Perhaps we could even communicate with other intelligent life in the distant reaches of the universe.

What this suggests to me is that instead of spending billions of dollars to land a person on Mars, which really won't tell us much that we don't already know, we might be much better off if we spent the same amount of money attempting to learn more about the Spirit World, and so unlock a whole new world of possibilities.

Chapter 14

Conclusion

Well, now that we have had two enjoyable trips together – one to the past, and one to the future – I think that it is time I tell you my conclusion regarding the reality of an Afterlife.

There is a well-known saying that "Beauty is in the eye of the Beholder." Based on my experience, I think that this is certainly true. A similar saying, that relates to our discussion of the Afterlife, is "Truth is in the mind of the Believer."

I don't think anyone living today on this earth knows for sure that there is an Afterlife, because the only person that we know of who died and was then resurrected is Jesus Christ. In fact, there are many persons living today who question the historical accuracy of this information about the life of Jesus, because they claim that in three days the body would have deteriorated so much that it would be impossible for it to be resurrected. I can understand why people may believe this, but if you accept the statement that I made in Chapter 5 that "...we can place no limitations on what God can do," then it is entirely possible that the body of Jesus could be resurrected after he had been dead for all that time. Surely the God who created the enormously complex body in the first place would have the ability to temporarily halt normal deterioration for as long as He wanted to.

In Chapter 1, I gave you some information about John Polkinghorne. I was really impressed with what he had to say, because he is highly qualified, both as a scientist and as a theologian. This was important to me, because I have a sincere belief that a melding between science and religion is where we need to head in the future to help us truly understand the mysteries of life. Here is what Dean Nelson says that Polkinghorne believes about the Afterlife:

"At 80, Polkinghorne doesn't let his own doubts keep him from believing, any more than he lets his doubts about quantum physics keep him from solving problems. He still prays, still celebrates the Eucharist, still believes in some kind of life eternal. As for belief in God, 'it's a reasonable position, but not a knock-down argument,' he said. 'It's strong enough to bet my life on it. I give my life to it, but I'm not certain. Sometimes I'm wrong.'"

Well, where does this leave me? I give Life Eternal a 99% chance of being a reality. In a few years after I cross over, I will know if my common sense analysis is correct.

Of course, just because I believe the Afterlife is almost a sure thing, I don't mean to suggest that I know a lot about the details of what immortal life will be like. It is my expectation, however, that with further scientific research about the Spirit World we will learn a lot that we do not know today, and this will help bridge the gap between those people living on the earth and those who have passed on to the Spirit World.

I hope that the thoughts I have expressed will be helpful to you as you travel on your faith journey. I am looking forward to hearing feedback from you.

In closing this chapter, I would like to repeat the admonition from Buddha that I quoted at the start of this book:

> *"Believe nothing, no matter where you read it, or who said it, not even if I have said it, unless it agrees with your own reason and common sense"*
>
> *- Buddha*

Well, I'm certain that Buddha was a much smarter person than I am, but we both agree that we should rely on our "common sense!"

Now I guess the ball is in your court. What does your "common sense" tell you?

Appendix 1

My Dream for Eliminating World Wars in the Future

When I started writing this book, my only goal was to prove that there was an Afterlife which nearly everyone would enjoy after they died and physically left this earth. I believe that I have been able to accomplish this goal with my "common sense" approach to this subject. As time went on, however, I realized that the world was in great peril due to our inability to eliminate wars, so I added another goal for my book: to come up with a plan that addressed the problem of World Wars.

It seems like ever since the dawn of civilization, mankind has periodically been involved in wars, and over the centuries these conflicts have become increasingly deadly. Now that we have nuclear weapons, we must eliminate wars in the future, or we may completely destroy our civilization as we know it.

In developing my dream for the future, I would like to take you back to June, 1942 when I joined the Radiation Laboratory at MIT as a Staff Member. The Radiation Laboratory, better known as Rad Lab, was started as a crash program to help win the war against Hitler in Europe. This lab functioned from October 1940 until December 31, 1945. Alfred Lee Loomis, a millionaire and physicist who headed his own private laboratory, selected the location for the laboratory on the campus at MIT, and he arranged funding for the Rad Lab until federal money was allocated. The head of the Rad Lab was Dr. Lee A. DuBridge.

Initially, the laboratory was staffed by eminent nuclear physicists who were on leaves of absence from universities throughout the United States. I was privileged to be in the first group of engineers who went to the lab at MIT directly after graduating from the universities that we were attending.

The Rad Lab was responsible for developing most of the 10 cm radar systems that were used during World War II, and the use of these systems has been credited as a major factor in winning the war against Hitler. Early in the war, we faced a serious problem when enemy submarines attacked our ships as they were supplying war materials to Europe. With the development of 10 cm radar systems, it became possible to scan the ocean with a relatively small radar dish that could be mounted in an airplane. This made it possible to see the conning towers of submerged submarines, so that they could then be bombed and destroyed.

Now it is 2015, and most of the people I knew at the Rad Lab are no longer living. God has been good to me, and fortunately I'm still alive and kicking, and still dreaming about the future of our country and the world.

Unfortunately, now that many nations have the capability of making and deploying atomic bombs, there is a serious danger that a rogue nation could start World War III. A war like this could eliminate most of civilization on this earth as we know it. Today, we already know of nations that say they hate the United States and feel that we should be destroyed, and also feel that Israel should be obliterated from the face of the earth. As we know, the Holocaust during World War II killed millions of Jewish people, and right after the war was over we said that we would never again let this happen. Yet in a relatively short period of time since the end of World War II, there is talk of what could be another Holocaust. This seems almost unbelievable to me, but it is a reality that I think we must face, and that is why I feel that it is vitally important to come up with a program that has the potential to ultimately result in the elimination of all future World Wars.

After doing considerable research on the Afterlife, I came to the conclusion that it truly does exist in what we call the Spirit World. We know very little about the Spirit World, but I believe that there is sufficient anecdotal evidence to "prove" that it really exists. As I've said before, we don't really understand how all people are connected together in the Spirit World, but it is my guess that communication there takes place instantaneously rather than at the relatively slow speed of electromagnetic communication.

If my assumption is correct, and I reiterate that this is just my guess at this point in time, then it would be possible that information from far reaches of our universe could instantly be transmitted from one end of our universe to the other.

As I indicated earlier in this book, we have spent literally billions of dollars to try and capture information from space, and also to land on some of the planets within our solar system. While all of this effort has given us some useful information, we have not as yet identified any type of "signals" that seem to be coming from intelligent life elsewhere. At this point it would be easy to conclude that there is no other intelligent life elsewhere, but my common sense tells me that this would be completely illogical.

If we were to set up a program to research the Spirit World, it could answer all the questions we have been pursuing about the true nature of the universe, and even provide insight into questions that, at this point, we don't even know how to ask. Of course this kind of research would take a lot of money, and the obvious question would be exactly where would this money come from?

As I was thinking about the problem of funding, I became curious as to just how many billionaires there are at this moment in the United States. *Forbes* magazine has compiled a list indicating that in 2015 there are 615 billionaires in the United States, with Bill Gates at the top of that list. *Forbes* goes on to list the billionaires by continents, and the grand total of billionaires in the world is 1,826. Almost every country is represented. It seems that most of these billionaires have foundations set up to handle the disbursement of money to various charities – or, perhaps, to fund research that could change the future of the human race.

Unfortunately, I do not personally know any billionaires, so I hope that at least one of them will read this book, and be interested in funding the proposed new research project that, for convenience at this point, I will call this the Spirit Lab project.

What is needed at this time is for someone to volunteer to be the Chairman of a Committee to design and propose the setup of the Spirit Lab. If I were 50 years younger I would be very interested in volunteering for this job, but at ninety-four years of age I no longer have the time or energy to tackle anything this ambitious. I would be glad, however, to serve as a member of a Committee that may be set up to accomplish this job. So, the critical thing at this time is to find a volunteer to get the ball rolling.

I believe that this project should be entirely funded by private funds rather than by any government. For one thing, I want to avoid any concern about the so-called "separation of church and state" that relates to the First Amendment of the US Constitution. Also, I think it would be wise to avoid the typical regulations that always seem to come up when government is involved. Initially, I would expect that all funds would come from US billionaires, but ultimately I would like to see some participation from around the world, because this project is of importance to all of humankind. I hope that eventually there could be a lot of support from ordinary people, most of whom may not be extremely wealthy. I think it is important that many people take "ownership" of this project.

Ideally, I believe that the project headquarters

should be located at some prestigious University in the US. I am fortunate to be an alumnus of two such schools; MIT, and Case Western Reserve University. Either of these universities would be an excellent location for our Spirit Lab. Of course, there are many other fine universities throughout the United States which would also be excellent locations.

I don't know how many staff members would initially be involved, but I think, to begin with we should anticipate having at least a dozen, along with a number of supporting personnel. Many of these staff members could be high-profile researchers on loan from other universities, but I feel we should also include some younger people, under age 30, as part of the staff. I receive the *MIT Technology Review* magazine, and also the Case Western Reserve University *Think* magazine, and I'm really impressed with what is being accomplished by scientists and engineers who are under 35 years of age.

We would need to have sufficient funds to pay everyone well, as these great minds would be pretty far up the "pay scale," and many of them would need to be temporarily dislocated from their present homes in order to join this new group of researchers at the Spirit Lab.

These people need to be carefully selected, and it is important that each of them have a belief in the possible existence of a Spirit World. A Gallup poll on immortality found that only 16% of leading scientists believed in life after death as opposed to anywhere from 67% to 82% of the general population, and only 4% of the scientists thought it might be possible for science to prove it. I was quite surprised when I read these statistics, and this just emphasizes to me how careful we need to be in selecting participants for this project.

As I am writing this, I have just received the September/October issue of the *MIT Technology Review* magazine. The lead article in this magazine is titled "35 Innovators Under 35." I have perused the articles about each of the 35 innovators, and none of them are involved in anything that even approaches the kind of research that I am suggesting about the Spirit World. I think that part of the problem is that there is still a stigma attached to this sort of investigation, because it deals with religious beliefs and is not "scientific" in nature. Having said this, however, I understand that there are a few universities and also private groups that are doing significant research on communication with the Spirit World.

Now I am not naïve enough to think that I am going to suddenly receive a phone call from some billionaire who will say, "Chuck, count me in for 100 million dollars." I think it will be a tough sell, because billionaires have so many organizations asking them for funds. I truly believe that we can get this project off the ground, however, because of my personal experience over many years, where the impossible happened in my life – thanks to the influence of God!

The critical first step is to find someone to be the Chairman of a blue-ribbon committee to get the project underway, and this is where I need help from the readers of this book. This could probably get started with 1 or 2 million dollars in funding. Wouldn't you like to be associated with a project that ultimately results in the elimination of all wars from our world?

If you are interested in playing a key role in my proposed Spirit Lab research program, or if you have friends who may be interested, please email me at chuck@chuckswartwout.com. I would very much appreciate any help or insight you may be able to contribute to the process of getting this program going.

So how do I know that if we are able to set up a research program, it will give us the answers we are looking for? Well, the answer is that I don't know, but I am a believer in the old adage "Nothing ventured, nothing gained." At this point, no one knows what will be discovered in this research program, but I strongly feel it is worth a try. As we know, God created human beings with amazing minds, and I think that He would be pulling for us to find the answers we were seeking! If there is the slightest possibility that the Spirit Lab project could be the start of a program that would eventually eliminate wars in the future, I think that this is an exciting prospect worth pursuing with every resource at our disposal!

Thanks for your consideration. I hope to hear from many of you.

God Bless You!

Chuck Swartwout

Appendix 2
Another Book

A Feedback Book™- You are one of the contributors!

Now it's your turn to join our "Town Hall" meeting ! I hope you have enjoyed reading my book, and I am really anxious to hear your thoughts, as I am a great believer in the collective wisdom of all of my readers. I hope that I will hear from many thousands of you. Here is how to proceed:

Click on my website, and when it opens up you'll see a menu item labeled, "Feedback." Click on this icon and you will then be able to enter your comments. There are a few ground rules that I would like to have you observe when you give me your feedback:

1. Please enter the date, your name or your initials, the city in which you live, and your email

address. For example, if I were entering a comment I would enter it like this: 9-25-15- Chuck Swartwout, Sedona, AZ - email –chuck@chuckswartwout.com Arizona.

2. Please keep your remarks as concise as possible. I hope to be able to read everyone's feedback, but this will only be possible if each response is concise. You will be able to see and read everyone's comments when you access my website, and if you wish, will be able to have dialog between yourself and other contributors. If things work out the way I hope, this will be like a big "Town Hall" meeting and we will all learn from each other.

3. Please, no profanity or other offensive comments.

4. It is my intention to archive these comments for future reference.

5. You agree to grant me the right to quote any of your comments in a future publication, without necessarily giving acknowledgment to you by name.

6. There is no guarantee that a second book will be published. This will depend upon the nature of the feedback that I receive, and my personal ability to write another book as I get closer to the day when I will personally "change channels"!

Appendix 3

Words to Live By

When we were creating our film, *Sedona the Spirit of Wonder*, we came across this wonderful poem written by an unknown Native American.

If we look at the path, we do not see the sky.
We are earth people
On a spiritual journey to the stars.
Our quest, our earth walk,
Is to look within, to know who we are,
To see that we are connected to all things,
That there is no separation,
Only in the mind.

Many years ago, Gretchen and I went on a camping trip to Death Valley, CA. While there we visited a fascinating place called Scotty's Castle. I walked up a hill to Scotty's grave, which overlooked the castle, and on his tombstone was the following epitaph:

Death Valley Scotty (Walter Scott)
1872 – 1934

I got four things to live by:
Don't say nothing that will hurt anybody
Don't give advice-Nobody will take it anyway
Don't complain – Don't explain

I thought that these were good admonitions for all of us to follow.

Here are some more:

Shoot for the moon . . . Even if you miss, you'll be among the stars. - Anonymous

If you can dream it, you can do it.
- Walt Disney

It is much easier to tame a wild idea than to invigorate one that has no life in the first place.
- Alex Osborne

Don't be afraid to take a big step if one is indicated. You can't cross a chasm in two small Jumps.
- David Lloyd George

If you want to do something and you feel in your bones that it's the right thing to do, do it! Intuition is often as important as the facts.
- H. Jackson Brown

If you only look at what is, you might never attain what could be. Success seems to be largely a matter of hanging on after others have let go.
- William Feather

One that meant the most to me was on a little plaque that my kids gave me many years ago:

A great man is he who has not lost the heart of a child.

No matter how old I get, I continue to strive to see God's wonderful universe with the same awe as a little child. It is too easy to take His magnificent creation for granted.

It is truly a miracle!

Acknowledgements

When I decided to write a book, one of the first people I contacted was Dean Nelson who is the head of the Journalism Department at Point Loma Nazarene University in San Diego, California. I read a book that he published about John Polkinghorne who has a fascinating background in both religion and science. This was of great interest to me, because I feel that this is the way we must go in the future to learn more about the Afterlife. I thank Dean Nelson for making me aware of John Polkinghorne's background.

A little later, I became a friend of Mark Ireland. He had written a book called *Soul Shift* which tells the tragic story of the sudden-death of his teenage son. Mark has been of great help and guidance to me after I started to write my book.

In writing my book, I decided to go the route of self-publishing. This appears to be the way that most authors go today. When I started to research this, I found that there were many companies that wanted to help me, but unfortunately, there were a lot of booby-traps I could fall into if I was not careful. I was very fortunate that I found Mike Ball to work with me as my editor and "Book Shepherd." Just like a real shepherd, my Book Shepherd has kept me from getting lost in the forest.

I thank Mike for the great help that he has been in getting my book completed and launched. He is an award-winning author and has a very broad experience in many fields, and has worked on many successful book programs.

Once the book is completed, then the important thing is to have an outstanding program of marketing. I am working with Scott Lorenz on this phase of the program, and I thank him for his expertise.

I thank my granddaughter, Roxanne Stehlik for her insight into the impact of other cultures in our world.

And last, but not least, I thank all the other members of my family, and my friends, who have encouraged me as I struggled to write my first book!

Bibliography

Academy of Spiritual & Consciousness Studies: *Afterlife Communication* – http://ascsi.org/conference/

Alexander, Eben. *Proof of Heaven.* New York: Simon & Schuster Paperbacks.

Annaton, Aleya. *The Technology of God.*

Anthony, Mark. *Evidence of Eternity.* Llwellyn Publications.

Bass, Diana Butler. *Christianity After Religion.* Harper One – Harper Collins Publishers.

Beischel, Judy. *From The Mouths of Mediums.*

Berlinski, David. *The Devils Delusion.* New York, Basic Books.

Bullivant, Richard. *True Time Travel Stories.*

Burpo, Todd. *Heaven Is for Real.* Nashville, Thomas Nelson.

Carson, Ben. *America the Beautiful.* Zondervan.

Carson, Ben. *One Nation*. Sentinel.

Childs, Annette. *Halfway Across the River*. The Wandering Feather Press.

DeStefano, Anthony. *A Travel Guide to Heaven*. Guideposts, New York.

Dowd, Michael. *Thank GOD for Evolution*. A Plume Book.

Eager, Rob. *Sell Your Book Like Wildfire*. Writer's Digest Books.

Fontana, David. *Is There An Afterlife?* O Books, USA.

Guggenheim, Bill & Judy. *Hello From Heaven*. New York: Bantam Books.

Hancock, Maureen. *The Medium Next Door.* Deerfield Beach, FL: Health Communications.

Hutchinson, Robert J. *The Politically Incorrect Guide to the Bible*. Regnery Publishing, Inc.

Ireland, Mark. *Messages from the Afterlife*. Berkeley, CA: North Atlantic Books.

Ireland, Mark. *Soul Shift*. Berkeley, CA: Frog Books.

Ireland, Richard. *Your Psychic Potential.* Berkeley, CA. North Atlantic Books.

Krasko, Genrich L. *This Unbearable Boredom of Being*. iUniverse, Inc.

Marks, Jeffrey A. *The Afterlife Interviews – Vol. 1.* Lynwood Washington: Arago Press.

Martin, Sharlene & Flacco, Anthony. *Publish Your Nonfiction Book.* Writer's Digest Books.

McLaren, Brian D. *Why Did Jesus, Moses, the Buddha, and Mohammed Cross the Road?* Jericho Books.

Mcluhan, Robert. *Randi's Prize.* Great Britain, Matador Publishing.

Moody, Jr., Raymond A. *Life After Life.* Harper, SanFrancisco.

Nelson, Dean & Giberson, Karl. *Quantum Leap.* Monarch Books. Oxford UK, & Grand Rapids, MI.

Olson, Bob. *Answers About the Afterlife.* Building Bridges Press.

Polkinghorne, John. *Quantum Physics & Theology* : Yale University Press.

Piper, Don. *90 Minutes in Heaven.* Guideposts, Baker Publishing Group, New York.

Reiser, Paul. *How to Get to Carnegie Hall*

Ritchie, George G. *Return from Tomorrow.* Guideposts, Baker Publishing Group, NY.

Schwartz, Gary E., Ph.D. *The Afterlife Experiments.* Atria Books, New York.

Schwartz, Gary E. *The Sacred Promise*. Atria Books, New York.

Schwartz, Robert. *Your Soul's Gift*. Whispering Winds Press.

Smith, Rick. *CreateSpace & Kindle Self-Publishing Masterclass*. Rick Smith.

Spong, John Shelby. *Eternal Life – A New Vision*. Harper Collins Publishers, New York.

Stefano, Anthony. *A Travel Guide To Heaven*. Guideposts, Doubleday, New York.

Swartwout, Charles J. *A Curiosity Box*. Swartwout Productions, Sedona, AZ.

Taylor, Greg. *Stop Worrying! There Probably Is An Afterlife*.

Weiss, Brian L. *Many Lives, Many Masters*. Simon & Schuster, New York, 2010.

Weiss, Brian. *Messages from the Masters*. Grand Central Publishing, New York, 2001.

Young, Stephen. *True Stories of Real Time Travelers*. Amazon Digital Services, Inc., 2014.

Web References

Academy of Spiritual & Consciousness Studies – ascsi.org

Mike Ball – *WriteItTight.com, MikeBallBooks.com*

Mark Ireland – *www.MarkIrelandAuthor.com*

Scott Lorenz – *Book-Marketing-Expert.com*

Dean Nelson – *DeanNelson.net*

Bob Olson – *www.BestPsychicDirectory.com*

Susanne Wilson – *CarefreeMedium.com*

Here's what people are saying about

You Don't Die – You Just Change Channels

A Common Sense Approach to a Not So Common Topic – the Afterlife

Not many engineers who know how to write would author a book attempting to prove the existence of an Afterlife. But Chuck Swartwout is no ordinary author, and is certainly no ordinary engineer. I found that out when I read his wonderful book, *You Don't Die – You Just Change Channels – A common sense guide to God our Creator and Eternity in Heaven.*

...You will not find Heaven, eternity, or the Afterlife discussed anywhere else as Swartwout does in this short, highly annotated, and very readable book.

... The author's discussion of eternity, the nature of God, Heaven and the Afterlife is easy to understand because he takes a common sense approach rather than a more traditional theological, doctrinal approach. It is a refreshing approach and, believe it or not, makes sense.

- *Emory Daniels*

Here's what people are saying about

You Don't Die – You Just Change Channels

A "common sense" look at the big questions that are, unfortunately, currently unanswerable.

At the beginning of Chuck Swartwout's intriguing and engaging spiritual exploration, *You Don't Die – You Just Change Channels*, the author confesses to being a dreamer. He says anyone who ever accomplished anything has been a "dreamer." The book is a journey through time investigating the possibility of a "spirit world," a place where our minds go when we die; a world of endless possibilities, connection and communication. Chuck Swartwout's literary debut at age 94 is a "common sense" look at the big questions that are, unfortunately, currently unanswerable. But it's also a passionate and inspiring call to action for more research into the most central questions about what happens to us when we die.

- John J. Kelly Cincinnati City Beat, Amazon Reviewer

Here's what people are saying about

You Don't Die – You Just Change Channels

A Common Sense Approach to an Eternal Question

"It is this kind of common senses approach to the controversial subject of Afterlife that make this one of the more accessible and reliable books yet written about the Very Big Questions. But to grow into Chuck Swartwout's Common Sense guide, the journey should be a personal one. This little book is a wonderful challenge to think in different ways. It's a gift from a learned gentle man with whom an evening stroll beneath the stars would be a great and illuminating experience and pleasure. Highly recommended."

- Grady Harp, Amazon Hall of Fame Reviewer

Made in the USA
Lexington, KY
14 March 2016